for
My big brother Dr. Mark who was n
a God-honoring man, husband an
more sway on my Christian journey tnan ne knows.

Mike Pettengill, *The Gospel Came to You*

© 2018 by Mike Pettengill

Cover and art design: Madison Pettengill

For additional information please visit www.TheGospelCameToYou.com.

Paperback ISBN: 978-0-9976623-6-8
Ebook ISBN: 978-0-9976623-7-5
PDF ISBN: 978-0-9976623-8-2

The Gospel Came to You:
Daily Reflections for Advent

For we know, brothers loved by God, that he has chosen you,
because our gospel came to you not only in word,
but also in power and in the Holy Spirit and with full conviction.
You know what kind of men we proved to be among you for your sake.
- 1 Thessalonians 1:4-5

Contents

Preface

The word "advent" comes from the Latin word "Adventus," and means "coming." The exact origin of the advent celebration is unknown, but versions of advent can be traced back to the fourth, fifth and sixth centuries. The details and dates of the practice of advent vary throughout history, geography and among the divisions within the Christian church. The consistent aspect of advent is its observance has always been a way to remember Jesus Christ.

In today's Western evangelical churches and homes advent is a rich and joyful celebration. It is used to commemorate the second coming of Jesus and to prepare the hearts of Christian disciples to celebrate the remembrance of the birth of our Savior. In our modern, busy lives advent is an opportunity for Christians to slow down and remember the real purpose for Christmas is not parties, gifts and ski trips, but is about honoring the birth of our risen King.

Modern advent is most commonly celebrated from the fourth Sunday before Christmas until Christmas Day. The first Sunday of advent can occur as early as November 27th or as late as December 3rd, but always includes the four Sundays before Christmas. Today's advent commemorations can (but do not always) include the Advent wreath, Jesse Tree or Advent calendar. The important point is the inclusion of study, prayer and worship of Jesus.

The commemoration of advent became important to my family when we moved from the United States to serve as fulltime missionaries. Wherever we lived during December, we witnessed that cultures around the globe celebrated Christmas differently. In addition, the Christmas season is a time when many missionaries feel homesick as they are away from friends, family and the aspects of Christmas which remind them of home. My wife once observed, "Decorating a Christmas tree just doesn't feel right when it is 90 degrees out with 90 percent humidity." One year, when there were no traditional Western Christmas trees in our adopted city, we decorated a Christmas palm tree. It simply didn't feel the same.

Advent devotionals became a valuable way for our missions family to remain focused on Jesus and to not forget why Christmas is so important. In those early years of our missions work .pdf or eBook versions of daily advent devotionals by John Piper, R.C. Sproul, John MacArthur and others saved much heartache for our family and the other missionaries around us.

For years I remembered the difficulty of those times and how valuable substantive Bible-based advent devotionals were to my family and other missionaries. Instead of simply thanking the authors and ministries who produced the advent devotionals my family used (which I have done) I assumed those Godly servants would rather I better

1

use my time to glorify God. I stand on the shoulders of giants and thank them by providing this advent devotional to you and your family.

Clearly, there are better advent devotionals than this. I would never be so bold as to claim this advent devotional breaks new ground or is better than others you could use during advent season. My hope is that through my prayer, hours of research and writing you and your family are impacted in a positive way. I pray I have been able to convey a Reformed and covenantal perspective of our Father's inerrant Word. God can certainly use this cracked vessel to bring himself glory, if he so chooses.

I started writing this advent devotional while I served as a missionary in Honduras and completed the writing while serving Jesus in Equatorial Guinea. The art, contained herein, is all original work produced by my daughter who served by my side in Honduras. It is my prayer you and your family receive benefit from this devotional and it brings you closer to our Father. If you do not have a saving relationship with Jesus Christ, I pray you drop to your knees before you continue reading and take the gift he has already given you. How much more sweet this advent season will be if it is your first within the body of Christ. I pray God receives glory from both my writing and your worship with this book.

May Jesus Christ be remembered well during this advent season and every day through his devoted disciples. Amen!

Day #1

Righteous Branch

"Behold, the days are coming, declares the Lord, when I will raise up for David a righteous Branch, and he shall reign as king and deal wisely, and shall execute justice and righteousness in the land."
- Jeremiah 23:5

The branch of a tree bears its fruit and sustains the life of the tree. The term branch holds great significance throughout the Bible. The term is used literally, symbolically and metaphorically over 100 times in Scripture. The branch referred to in this passage will ultimately bear fruit which will unite God with his people forever.

We understand Jeremiah's prophecy to be of the Messiah who is called the branch. Here the anticipated Messiah is called the righteous branch, not only because he himself was righteous, but because he will make his people righteous. The author is holding out hope that the remnant of the flock will be re-gathered, and God will put a new and righteous king on David's throne.

The promises contained in the Old Testament hinge on the coming of the Messiah who would rule as king from the line of David. It was promised that he would conquer the enemies of God's people and bring righteousness and peace for all eternity. The Messiah would usher in all of God's promises.

The followers of Christ have great assurance God has honored his covenant with David and Jesus is the righteous Branch which grafts believers into a relationship with the Creator. Jesus is the foretold Messiah. Jeremiah, who served as both a priest and prophet, foretold of the coming Messiah nearly six centuries before the birth of Jesus. Two thousand years later Christians gain great assurance in knowing it is our Lord who fulfilled the prophecy and reigns today as King.

ଔ

"'He will be great and will be called the Son of the Most High. And the Lord God will give to him the throne of his father David, and he will reign over the house of Jacob forever, and of his kingdom there will be no end.'"
- Luke 1:32-33

"How many observe Christ's birthday! How few, his precepts! O! 'tis easier to keep Holidays than Commandments." - Benjamin Franklin

PRAY: thank you God for establishing prophecy of the Messiah and thousands of years later fulfilling that prophecy with the arrival of your son Jesus. Thank you for connecting your son to the royal and priestly lineage of Israel and thus adding us, his disciples, into the heredity of your elect people.

Sure Law

"The law of the Lord is perfect, reviving the soul; the testimony of the Lord is sure,
making wise the simple"
- Psalm 19:7

One day a man complained to Mark Twain that the Bible was all mixed up, conflicted, and filled with passages he could not comprehend. Twain replied, "I have more difficulty with the passages I do understand than with the passages I do not understand."

Two of the most important points about the law are; it is perfect and it is from God. God's gospel is a complete plan for merciful salvation, describing for the sinner all that his retched life has earned him, but what Christ agreed to pay in his stead. There are no unneeded or redundant points in the Word of God. All man needs to receive eternity by the Father's side is contained in God's merciful Bible.

God knitted together his creation and his law. This union eagerly awaited the redemptive role Jesus would play as the intermediary between the Creator and the created. No authority affirms the Bibles validity, because no lesser source can address the perfect elements of the Word of our Father. Only the Bible can sufficiently prove itself.

In Paul's second letter to Timothy he instructs the young Christians in Ephesus that every word in Scripture is a gift to us from God which is appropriate to be used to educate, rebuke, guide and instruct the followers of Christ. For millennia the intellectuals of the world have debated, in great depths, every complex facet of God. However, a simple person who looks toward heaven for truth finds purer wisdom than the great minds combined. Our compassionate God gave us the Bible as a gift to help point us to his son.

ଔ

"At that time Jesus declared, 'I thank you, Father, Lord of heaven and earth, that you have hidden these things from the wise and understanding and revealed them to little children;'"
- Matthew 11:25

"The story is about God's Son in the fullness of time being sent by the heavenly Father into this world." - Ligon Duncan

ℬℬ

PRAY: Heavenly Father thank you for the gift of your perfect law to your creation. We give thanks knowing, through your law, you have provided your children with examples of how we may show love to you and you have provided us with examples of why we so desperately need Jesus Christ to fulfill the law.

One Shepherd

"And I will set up over them one shepherd, my servant David, and he shall feed them: he shall feed them and be their shepherd."
- Ezekiel 34:23

In the Western world we are less familiar with the relationships which exist between a shepherd and his sheep. Shepherds are known to sing to and talk to their sheep. They spend hours at a time with the sheep. The shepherd will nudge them in the right direction and pull them from danger. Shepherds will even risk their own lives to protect their sheep. The sheep trust and respond to their shepherd. A flock will only respond to the voice and presence of their shepherd and no other.

God did not want Israel to have a human king. He desired for his people to be different, to rely on their perfect Father who would provide them with all their needs. Instead, Israel demanded a human champion like other nations. God provided his petulant children with David, a man after God's own heart, but his people wanted Saul, a tall, attractive leader. After the failed experiment with Saul, David ruled over Israel. David was a sinner and made poor decision, but he ruled with God's people in mind. David prayed for his people and asked God to punish him, instead of Israel. David, like the rest of us, sinned against God, but always returned to repent and seek God's glory. David always loved and cared for God's people.

David was God's chosen shepherd over his beloved people. David was a foreshadowing of Jesus Christ. Jesus is the good shepherd who laid down his life for his sheep. The Son was sent to guide, direct and train us into a saving relationship with the Father. Christ was sent to lay down his life so God's followers could be spared. Like a shepherd standing between a bear and his sheep, Jesus placed himself between us and an eternity separated from the Father.

☙

"And I have other sheep that are not of this fold. I must bring them also, and they will listen to my voice. So there will be one flock, one shepherd."
- John 10:16

"Jesus was God and man in one person, that God and man might be happy together again." - George Whitefield

❧

PRAY: loving Creator, we acknowledge our desperate need for the perfect Shepherd. It is our own nature which necessitates Jesus to stand between us and our sin and to protect us from ourselves. Thank you for sending Christ and the Spirit to watch over your sheep which you love so dearly.

Day #4

Faultless Forgiveness

"bearing with one another and, if one has a complaint against another, forgiving each other; as the Lord has forgiven you, so you also must forgive."
- Colossians 3:13

A late night TV show asked parents to trick their kids and video the response. The parents hid their children's Halloween candy and "confessed" they had eaten it all. As expected most children responded with screaming, hitting, and flopping to the floor. But, one little girl smiled and responded, "Mommy that makes me really sad...maybe next year we can share my candy...you can make it up to me by spending some time with me." Hundreds of children expressed what is in all of our hearts, and one little girl shared what is in Jesus' heart.

God forgives us, even though we had no cause to sin against him. We must forgive others as God has forgiven us. Gossip and hurtful words stir up evil and grieve the Spirit of God. While we were still sinners God reconciled us to himself. He did not first make us sinless. We too are to understand that those with whom we are to reconcile are sinners, yet still beautiful to God.

A man renewed by the blood of Christ acts upon new principles. The believer is created with a new heart. He is created in Jesus for the purpose of doing good works. We should strive toward the beauty of reconciliation for the glory of God. Biblical reconciliation begins with one person talking directly to the person who offended him. Reconciliation glorifies God, while an angry, bitter heart robs him of his glory. God's glory is always more important than our ease and comfort.

Jesus reconciled sinful man with perfect God. Without the blood of Christ, we are eternally separated from the Father. No individual's actions against you could ever be as heinous as your sins against God. If God lovingly forgives us we should glorify him by sharing forgiveness with others.

CR

"Who is a God like you, pardoning iniquity and passing over transgression for the remnant of his inheritance? He does not retain his anger forever, because he delights in steadfast love."
- Micah 7:18

"If we could condense all the truths of Christmas into only three words, these would be the words: 'God with us.'" - John MacArthur

PRAY: compassionate Jesus, we thank you for forgiving all our sins when we had no cause to sin against you. Your mercy saves us and provides the perfect example of how we should interact with others. Erase from us the sin of pride which prevents us from truly forgiving those who have wronged us.

Humble Servant

"Hear now, O Joshua the high priest, you and your friends who sit before you, for they are men who are a sign: behold, I will bring my servant the Branch. For behold, on the stone that I have set before Joshua, on a single stone with seven eyes, I will engrave its inscription, declares the Lord of hosts, and I will remove the iniquity of this land in a single day."
- Zechariah 3:8-9

In 1956 five humble missionaries entered the jungles of Ecuador to evangelize the murderous Huaorani Indians. Two days after first contact the Huaorani murdered all five men. If the story ended there it would be tragic. Decades later we learn the Huaorani came to Christ in great numbers because of their interaction with those five servants of God. Also, the retelling of their story in magazines, books and movies has inspired thousands of new missionaries into service. These martyrs served with distinction.

The prophecy from the prophet Zechariah combines two names for the foretold Messiah. He is referred to as both the Servant and the Branch. This Servant Branch will remove sin from the world in one day. What a Servant indeed. This Servant, from the almost extinct royal line of David, would serve like none other.

Jesus entered this world, not in luxury, but surround by animal dung. He didn't live a life of means, but as an unassuming carpenter. He was not honored as nobility by religious leaders, but arrested. He was not treated to fine dining by authorities, but tortured and killed. As the Son of God, Jesus deserved respect, tribute and worship. He knew before he came to earth he was coming to serve and supply salvation for the unworthy. His crucifixion was the most selfless form of service man has ever seen.

This suffering servant, this willing sacrifice, Jesus was sent to free the captives and provide sight to the blind. Jesus Christ demonstrated service, one of the gifts of the Spirit, to perfection. The New Testament is clear what our response should be to hearing of this service by Christ. We are to serve others as Christ has served us and we are to follow in his steps in glorifying God by our actions.

❧

"He has no need, like those high priests, to offer sacrifices daily, first for his own sins and then for those of the people, since he did this once for all when he offered up himself."
- Hebrews 7:27

"The Son of God became a man to enable men to become the sons of God." - C.S. Lewis

꒰∽◦≫꒱

PRAY: our humble King, we marvel at the historical fact you diminished your position from the exalted throne of heaven to a mere baby among sinners. While the human kings of the world lavish themselves in riches you came to serve your subordinates. Our almighty Lord became a modest servant for us.

Day #6

Limitless Mercy

"he saved us, not because of works done by us in righteousness, but according to his own mercy, by the washing of regeneration and renewal of the Holy Spirit,"
- Titus 3:5

A middle-aged Pastor was mentoring a teenage boy while sitting in a booth of a country restaurant. The boy asked him to explain the Christian faith. The man said, "Christianity is when you get something for nothing." Sitting in the booth next to them was a little old lady who had spent her entire life in service of the Lord. She overheard the Pastor's response and interrupted, "I'm so sorry to have eavesdropped on you young man, but you are wrong. A relationship with our Savior is so much more than that. Christianity is when we receive everything for nothing."

Our salvation does not stem from our works or actions. In us there is an utter absence of the ability for righteous works to be done. Only God can do good. Our actions do not influence God. We cannot earn nor do we deserve heaven. Neither abstaining from actions, nor performing good works earns us merit with the Creator. Even saying we "accepted Christ" places the decision in our hands.

The Lord saved us, we did not save ourselves. God must first act before salvation can occur. Our salvation is a result of God's limitless mercy. God's gift of mercy cleanses our sin and provides us with a new spirit. We are so corrupt, not only are we unable to save ourselves, we don't have the ability to choose God. His mercy and love toward us is the cause of our salvation. Even our faith in Jesus is a gift from God.

Our salvation is a result of God's works and his mercy. When we try to take credit for contributing to our salvation we rob our Savior of the glory he deserves. God's absolute mercy engulfs our lives and is the most amazing gift a sinner can receive.

℞

"Have mercy on me, O God, according to your steadfast love; according to your abundant mercy blot out my transgressions."
- Psalm 51:1

13

"Jesus Christ was not first a man upon whom divinity descended. He was first God who took upon Himself humanity." - R. Fowler White

PRAY: our merciful Lord, we do good works and show mercy to others and look inward at our sinful hearts with pride. True mercy comes from you and is given to the lost so they can see your majesty. Give us hearts inclined toward your glory and away from our sin to help us to share the mercy you have given us with others.

Foretold Birth

"But you, O Bethlehem Ephrathah, who are too little to be among the clans of Judah, from you shall come forth for me one who is to be ruler in Israel, whose coming forth is from of old, from ancient days."
- Micah 5:2

Biblical scholars estimate there are hundreds of Messianic prophecies in the Old Testament which point to Jesus. The Old Testament focuses us on Jesus and prepares the world for his coming.

In the small town of Bethlehem, in the district of Ephrathah, located five miles south of Jerusalem, and 2,500 feet above sea level, an amazing miracle was prophesied. Bethlehem was the birthplace of David and later Jesus Christ. God used the decree of a Roman Emperor to coax Joseph and Marry to Bethlehem and fulfill this prophecy. The prophet Micah identifies not only the fact that Israel's Messiah will come, but from what city he will be born. God, in great detail and great splendor, rolled out the details of the birth of Jesus 700 years before the actual event.

The prevailing sovereignty of God controlled all of the complex facts to orchestrate an amazing miracle. God commands both heaven and earth. He turned the hearts of rulers to do his will. He guided the act and timing of the census. He directed the birthplace of Joseph a generation before Jesus. He controlled the timing of Mary's pregnancy. All this to coordinate the miracle that Jesus would be born in Bethlehem to fulfill prophecy. Jesus Christ would be born so save an unworthy race. Jesus is not a common man whose origin was experienced in time as we know it. He came forth "from of old." Jesus is the One who was mentioned "from ancient of days." Christ is the eternal Son of God.

In this foretelling of the coming Messiah the prophet Micah shows future generations their God will forever expand his own glory, keep the promises he makes and act in the best interest of his followers.

ෲ

"Has not the Scripture said that the Christ comes from the offspring of David, and comes from Bethlehem, the village where David was?"
- John 7:42

"The greatest and most momentous fact which the history of the world records is the fact of Christ's birth." - Charles H. Spurgeon

PRAY: expected King, for millennia man was told you were coming and of your miraculous birth. You came into this world as you said you would and accomplished exactly what you promised. So many of your creation still do not see you for what you are. Give us hearts to reach the lost in your name.

Day #8

Always Present

"For where two or three are gathered in my name, there am I among them."
- Matthew 18:20

Can you be a Christian without going to church? Yes, your salvation is secure. But, a Christian who doesn't attend church is like a kettledrum player without an orchestra, a baseball pitcher without a team, a politician on a deserted island, or a sailor without a ship. It just doesn't make sense.

Jewish custom required a minimum of 10 men to form a synagogue or to hold public prayer. Jesus promised he would be present in an even smaller gathering. Only, "two or three witnesses" need be gathered in his name for him to be with them. Jesus affirms he will be divinely in attendance. He desires to be among his disciples as they seek to glorify him. Jesus being present during our gatherings not only shows his love and desire to communion with his followers, but it also confirms the omnipresence expected of the Son of God.

Corporate worship and corporate prayer are a cornerstone of the historic Christian church. Accountability to fellow believers is a major reason, as is the ability to learn how to worship from others. Christ felt corporate worship was so important he promised to be in attendance at each and every occasion. At every worship service, at every gathering for prayer or study, at every missions committee meeting, at every church leadership meeting, the Creator is present, Christ himself attends. When we neglect regular public gatherings of fellow believers, we forgo the opportunity to be in the presence of the King of kings.

Do not overlook the blessed opportunities to worship, serve and study in communion with your blessed Savior.

ଔ

"Sing and rejoice, O daughter of Zion, for behold, I come and I will dwell in your midst, declares the LORD. And many nations shall join themselves to the LORD in that day, and shall be my people. And I will dwell in your midst, and you shall know that the LORD of hosts has sent me to you."
- Zechariah 2:10-11

17

"Let's resist the devil this Christmas with all the power of God by putting on the new nature Christ came to create." - John Piper

PRAY: Abba Father, you are worthy to glorify. Help us to see you as the involved, loving Father you are. Too often we view you only at the cosmic level and wrongly see you as disinterested in our daily lives. You have told us you love us and we intimately matter to you. Guide us to see you as present in all we do.

Coming Messenger

"Behold, I send my messenger, and he will prepare the way before me. And the Lord whom you seek will suddenly come to his temple; and the messenger of the covenant in whom you delight, behold, he is coming, says the Lord of hosts."
- Malachi 3:1

ೂಲ

James Montgomery was born in 18th century Scotland. He struggled through a difficult early life. His parents were martyred missionaries, he flunked out of school, he failed as a baker, storekeeper and author. In his 20s he was imprisoned twice on charges of sedition. Even through his early struggles Montgomery clung to the mercies of Christ. As an adult he sought to share that mercy with others. He worked tirelessly to end slavery, reform child labor laws, serve the poor and expand foreign missions.

At the age of 45 Montgomery wrote the Christmas carol "Angels from the Realms of Glory." In that carol Montgomery echoed the prophecies in Malachi 3:1 when he wrote, "Saints, before the altar bending, watching long in hope and fear, suddenly the Lord, descending, in His temple shall appear. Come and worship, come and worship, worship Christ the new-born King."

Montgomery beautifully ties together the old and new of the Messiah. Malachi, written 500 years before the birth of Christ, foretells of both John the Baptist ("the messenger") and Christ ("the Lord whom you seek"). Placing Malachi's future tense prophecy ("will suddenly come to his temple") and Montgomery's present tense praise ("worship Christ the new-born King") in the same context draws a wonderful picture for us. Malachi was the final inspired prophet in the Old Testament who proclaimed the advent of the Messiah in the New Testament.

When we worship Jesus Christ we are simultaneously praising his merciful prophecies, miraculous birth, grace filled death and cleansing resurrection. Christ was, is and always will be.

ભ

"This is he of whom it is written, 'Behold, I send my messenger before your face, who will prepare your way before you.'"
- Matthew 11:10

"All the Christmas presents in the world are worth nothing without the presence of Christ." - David Jeremiah

PRAY: our prophetic Word, you were present from the beginning. The Messiah existed at creation and then, as you promised, you sent him in the form of your son to separate us from our sin. You said you would send the herald of peace and indeed he reigns in our lives today.

Risen Judge

"because he has fixed a day on which he will judge the world in righteousness by a man whom he has appointed; and of this he has given assurance to all by raising him from the dead."
- Acts 17:31

A U.S. military veteran was having trouble adjusting to civilian life. He masked his PTSD with alcohol which got him in trouble with the law. The veteran found himself again in court for violating parole. The judge, also a military veteran, had compassion for the man, but the law demanded punishment. The judge sentenced the man to 24 hours in jail and then served the sentence by the man's side. Our eternal judge, Jesus Christ, has found us guilty. Instead of serving our sentence with us, he bore our punishment and declared us blameless.

Jesus was appointed by God to rise from the dead to not only be a strong philosopher or leader of governments. Jesus was selected to judge every human in history.

To our craven hearts the concept of being judged by anyone is repugnant. The post-modern man argues nobody should be judged. Live and let live many in our society might say. Plus, by who's standard should we be judged? Our modern relativism tells us there is no moral absolute. But, in these verses Paul tells the reader the risen and sinless Jesus, the only one in history worthy of evaluating anyone, will judge all of mankind in his righteousness. Without the blood of Christ, this is a standard to which no man can be found innocent.

Indeed, the entire world sits in judgement and is guilty of wickedness. Every man is worthy of eternal death. But, Jesus was sent, not simply to judge, but to serve the sentence as our substitute. The risen judge finds us guilty and declares us faultless through his own blood. By the sacrifice of Jesus Christ, we are seen by God as without iniquity.

❧

"before the LORD, for he comes, for he comes to judge the earth. He will judge the world in righteousness, and the peoples in his faithfulness."
- Psalm 96:13

"The more you think about it, the more staggering it gets. Nothing in fiction is so fantastic as this truth of the Incarnation." - J.I. Packer

PRAY: our Holy Advocate, only you are just and only you are worthy to save and condemn. Your followers have supreme confidence you are the perfect mediator between us and God. We thank you that through your compassion and for your glory you serve justice on some and mercy on others.

Rejoicing Jehovah

"The Lord your God is in your midst, a mighty one who will save; he will rejoice over you with gladness; he will quiet you by his love; he will exult over you with loud singing."
- Zephaniah 3:17

Love is a feeling which creates varying responses in different people. For the love of another many of us have responded in ways which are abnormal for our character. Love for another makes us giddy and jubilant. When we think of the character of God few of us would classify him as a singer. Yet, Zephaniah tells the reader God loves and rejoices over you to such a depth our Lord burst into song. How God must adore you to sing of his love for you.

The truth of the gospel would be absurd if not for the fact that it is glorious and perfect and true. The one true and perfect God desired to be reconciled with his flawed and sinful creation. Due to our sinful hearts we cannot turn to him, nor could his perfect nature allow him to commune with us. To resolve this problem, God sent his perfect son to suffer and to pay the penalty for our sins. Only after such a sacrifice can we have community with God.

The thanks we give to God for his sacrifice is to continue sinning. Yet, God does not turn from us, nor does he punish us for our ungratefulness. He rejoices over us with gladness. God does not lose heart in man nor turn from him. God responds to your rebelliousness by loving you and exalting over you.

How glorious it is to be loved so deeply by another. How rich it feels to know the love of another for us is so weighty it drives them to song. How much more profound it is to know the one who loves you in this way is the Creator of the universe.

છ

"And I heard a loud voice from the throne saying, 'Behold, the dwelling place of God is with man. He will dwell with them, and they will be his people, and God himself will be with them as their God.'"
- Revelation 21:3-4

"For the Christ-child who comes is the Master of all; No palace too great, no cottage too small." - Phillips Brooks

೦೦

PRAY: joyful Redeemer, your wrath and your joy are inseparable. You hate the wicked and you love the elect. Too frequently our simple and sinful hearts find difficulty in reconciling the many facets of your perfect nature. Give us the faith to worship you as you are and not as we desire you to be.

Day #12

Wise Spirit

"And the Spirit of the Lord shall rest upon him, the Spirit of wisdom and understanding, the Spirit of counsel and might, the Spirit of knowledge and the fear of the Lord."
- Isaiah 11:2

ॐ

The Lord sought a man after his own heart to lead Israel. When David was anointed as King the Holy Spirit rushed upon him and remained with him. David, this King with a heart similar to God's and empowered by the Holy Spirit, points to this passage in Isaiah and foreshadows the messianic leadership of Jesus.

Isaiah tells of the future Messiah who will be empowered by the Holy Spirit and emboldened for counsel and leadership. The Christ is promised to receive wisdom, understanding, counsel, might, knowledge and fear of the Lord. What a compassionate and qualified leader he will be. What a Savior he is. With these Spirit given qualifications Jesus is the leader who rules the earth effectively with justice and mercy.

Jesus possesses perfect wisdom and understanding of all things to qualify him to be the flawless teacher and governor of mankind. He maintains the forethought to depart faultless counsel to those who have faith in him. Christ holds the might of all the world's armies to enforce his decrees. Jesus encompasses the perfect knowledge of the will of God to rule with the wisdom surpassing the combined intellect of the world's leaders. Jesus seeks his own unmitigated glory with every decision. These characteristics prophesied in Isaiah and personified in Jesus establish the only Messiah.

As man debates and wrestles with the presidents and potentates of world governments, how blessed are the disciples of Jesus Christ to peacefully rest in the knowledge the Holy Spirit has bestowed upon our True Leader the perfect characteristics needed to govern his subjects in perfection.

℞

"how God anointed Jesus of Nazareth with the Holy Spirit and with power. He went about doing good and healing all who were oppressed by the devil, for God was with him."
- Acts 10:38

25

"The Scriptures systematically strip away the veneer that covers the real truth of the Christmas story." - Sinclair Ferguson

PRAY: dearest sovereign God, we acknowledge your unimaginable wisdom. Give us a taste of your wisdom by helping us to relinquish our lives to the Holy Spirit. Guide us each day to cede our hearts to the understanding and omnipotent Trinity so that our lives may be lived out in your will and for your glory.

High Priest

"Now the point in what we are saying is this: we have such a high priest, one who is seated at the right hand of the throne of the Majesty in heaven, a minister in the holy places, in the true tent that the Lord set up, not man."
- Hebrews 8:1-2

A fax machine is a tool used by businessmen to send replicas of documents from one place to another. A faxed paper, no matter how advanced the technology, produces a modest duplicate of the original. A faxed document is inferior, in every way, to the original. In the same fashion, interaction with a human priest produces inferior worship in comparison to communing directly with God. No matter how well intentioned, the intercession of a priest is like a faxed version of the original.

Jesus Christ, who is the high priest, is the completion of what was foretold in the Old Testament prophecy. Jesus is our personal high priest and minister and he sits at God's right hand. The tabernacle, a tent made by man, served only as a symbol of being close to God. Jesus actually resides in God's presence in heaven.

Jesus, as our priest, sits above the Levitical priests of the old covenant thus showing the supremacy of the new covenant. This concept that man could commune directly with Christ was a shock to the Old Testament Jews and the Jewish converts to Christianity, as well as religious leaders today. As disciples of Christ we interact directly with the chief priest. No mediator stands between us and our Lord.

The high priests of old and religious clergy today have been limited to the manmade facsimile of the holy of holies. Clerics, priests, and holy men are simply that; men. Men who, throughout the ages, have only entered man's best representations of holy temples. No matter how ornate or well-intentioned these shrines have all been only attempts to bring worshipers closer to God. Jesus Christ, our Savior and high priest, receives our prayers and petitions from within God's actual dwelling place.

ଔ

"Now Moses used to take the tent and pitch it outside the camp, far off from the camp, and he called it the tent of meeting. And everyone who sought the LORD would go out to the tent of meeting, which was outside the camp."
- Exodus 33:7

"Christmas is fast approaching. And now that Christ has aroused our seasonal expectations, he'll soon fulfill them all!" - Augustine

PRAY: personal High Priest, we exalt and worship you and are elated to know we can speak directly to you. You desire a personal relationship with your creation. No man or sect need ever come between us. Help us embrace our unencumbered relationship with our Savior and long to commune with you.

Everlasting God

"Before the mountains were brought forth, or ever you had formed the earth and the world, from everlasting to everlasting you are God."
- Psalm 90:2

Sponges near Antarctica are believed to be 10,000 years old. A pine tree has lived more than 5,000 years. A mollusk once lived 507 years. An Aldabra giant tortoise lived an estimated 255 years. The oldest recorded human lived 122 years. The oldest Asian elephant lived to be 86 years. The longest living domestic cat lived 38 years. God created these items and caused the time and matter which governs them to exist.

In this psalm, the only psalm attributed to Moses, the author cries to God to have mercy following an unnamed catastrophe. Moses discusses the weakness of man and asks God to reveal his mercy.

Moses recognizes God existed before the mighty mountains and even before the earth itself. He praises his Savior as being all powerful and capable of impacting our lives. Surely God, the Creator of all, could positively influence the lives of a few thousand mortal Israelites.

Moses calls God "everlasting to everlasting." God's existence has no beginning nor end. He is free from the constraints of time, and he created time itself. To juxtapose this description of God alongside the lives of Moses' people seems quite inconsequential. Why would a being so infinitely boundless and powerful, give a thought about the puny, insignificant lives of men?

Infinitely more improbable than imagining God cares about the comings and goings of man is the reality that he actually does care. The Creator of time, space and life desperately loves us. God knows you and you matter to him. God, of unimaginable power and influence, desperately desires to have a relationship with you. God so loved you he sent Jesus to reconcile you to himself. Only a God so big could envision such a plan. Only a God so loving could execute such a proposal.

"But we impart a secret and hidden wisdom of God, which God decreed before the ages for our glory."
- 1 Corinthians 2:7

"Jesus' coming is the final and unanswerable proof that God cares." - William Barclay

PRAY: our eternal Father, your wisdom is boundless and your counsel is perfect. The fact you would lower yourself to the level of man and love us is inconceivable. You existed before time and are without measure and you desire the perfect relationship with imperfect man.

Life Giver

"The thief comes only to steal and kill and destroy. I came that they may have life
and have it abundantly."
- John 10:10

Our post-modern consumer culture tries to convince us we deserve anything we want and should demand it now. At every turn we are told, "you deserve a break," "have it your way," "just do it," and "you're worth it." By contrast, Jesus has come to give us an abundant life today and for all eternity.

Jesus came to earth to live a sinless life and be sacrificed to pay the price for all our sins so we can live eternally in a relationship with God. Jesus tells us he came to give us life. The everlasting life does not begin upon our death, but Jesus desires for us an abundant life beginning now, on earth.

In heaven there is no death, no pain and God wipes our tears. There is no need for stars, moon or sun because the radiance from God is sufficient. Hatred, sorrow and disease will not exist in heaven. Justice will have been served, our sanctification will be complete and we will be able to glorify God in all.

Scripture does not promise a perfect life for Christian disciples on earth. In fact, those who follow Christ are promised persecution in this life. Yet, Christ still desires our abundant life to begin now, in this world. This abundant earthly life is not lived without pain, but is lived in the knowledge of the love Christ has for us. As we live for and in Jesus and live to glorify him through our words and actions we have within our grasp the ability to experience his mercy and grace today.

Our perfect life begins in heaven. Our joyful life lived in the love of Christ begins when we embrace our God glorifying sanctification and live in unity for the glory of Jesus.

ॐ

"You crown the year with your bounty; your wagon tracks overflow with abundance."
- Psalm 65:11

"Some businessmen are saying that this could be the greatest Christmas ever. I thought the first one was." - Hal Roach

PRAY: gracious Creator, your creatures pine for wealth and false security. You give eternal life to us and yet, we covet things of lesser value. Help us not to esteem that which in temporary over that which is permanent. Give us hearts which crave more for you and less for the world.

Rich Grace

"so that in the coming ages he might show the immeasurable riches of his grace in kindness toward us in Christ Jesus."
- Ephesians 2:7

John was raised by a Christian mother who taught him to read and memorize the Bible. She died when John was seven and for the next two decades he embraced a life of sin. Through his teens and into his 20s John became a troublemaker. He was kicked out of the Royal Navy and later became a slave trader. Following his conversion to Christianity he walked away from his reprobate life and into the church. As a minister, while preparing for a sermon on 1 Chronicles 17:16-17, John penned a biographical hymn to be sung during service. The hymn written by the ex-slave trader turned preacher begins, "Amazing grace! how sweet the sound, that saved a wretch like me! I once was lost, but now am found, was blind, but now I see."

John Newton's hymn captures the heart of every sinner who first comprehends the rich grace bestowed by God to an unworthy beggar. When a disciple of Christ first comprehends how he is experiencing the goodness, compassion and loving kindness of Christ it pierces his heart as it did John Newton's when he penned Amazing Grace. The Christian who is shown the steadfast love and favor of Jesus can only ask, how a good God could have diminished himself to save, "a wretch like me?"

No religion or school of thought, past or present, shows a focus on divine grace as does Christianity. False cults, sects and religions focus on man's sacrifice to an unreachable god and trying to win his favor. Christianity stands alone as we follow a Savior who freely diminishes himself to give what we could never earn. "Amazing grace, how sweet the sound."

☙

"Remember your mercy, O LORD, and your steadfast love, for they have been from of old."
- Psalm 25:6

"Not what we have been, not what we have done, but the Grace of God in Jesus Christ our Lord." - Martyn Lloyd Jones

PRAY: God of all grace, you have reached down to give us a gift we did not earn nor do we deserve. You give knowing we are incapable of repaying your love and generosity. Provide us opportunities to thank you for the grace you have given us by allowing us to share your grace and mercy with others.

New Covenant

"Behold, the days are coming, declares the Lord, when I will make a new covenant
with the house of Israel and the house of Judah,"
- Jeremiah 31:31

Try to envision a manmade contract which plays out like the covenant enacted by God. Would your landscaper or auto mechanic tolerate a contract change like the Creator of the Universe implemented? Imagine, you are going out with your spouse, so you call your favorite babysitter to watch the kids. You really like this babysitter so you offer to pay her $10,000 for the night, cater a fancy French meal for her and her friends and buy her a new wardrobe. In exchange she will watch your kids for four hours. She shows up and as you walk out the door the babysitter says, "You could never live up to your end of the contract, so I am changing it. I will watch your kids and I will pay you $100,000, fly you to Paris and when you get home I will have built you a new 10,000 sq. ft. house. Just say thanks and have a good time."

Not only is that story unbelievable, it really isn't good theology. The truth is, until glory, we will never grasp what Christ has done for us. Israel was given a covenant by God which they could never follow. The sinful heart of a man could never love God like he deserves. That covenant with Israel showed the importance of the promised Messiah. When he sent Jesus he eliminated the old covenant and established a new covenant. God said to man, "You love my son and I will do all the work."

In this new covenant Jesus endures the pain, humiliation, disgrace and dishonor by coming to earth, living among us, suffering, being sacrificed and dying. God loved us so much he eliminated the unmanageable covenant and gave us a new one where we embrace the eternal win-win scenario.

CR

"Therefore he is the mediator of a new covenant, so that those who are called may receive the promised eternal inheritance, since a death has occurred that redeems them from the transgressions committed under the first covenant."
- Hebrews 9:15

"That the Creator himself comes to us and becomes our ransom - this is the reason for our rejoicing." - Martin Luther

PRAY: God of the covenant, you paid the ultimate price to make us sinless and perfect in God's eyes. You created a covenant with your elect which enables us to embrace Jesus and have a relationship with you now and for all eternity. Without your payment we could never live a life worthy of our Lord.

Perfect Gift

"Every good gift and every perfect gift is from above, coming down from the Father of lights with whom there is no variation or shadow due to change."
- James 1:17

The Holy of Holies was the inner room of the Tabernacle where the Ark of the Covenant resided. It was a small (15' x 15') completely dark inner room. Nobody, but he high priest, could see inside nor enter it. The Holy of Holies was where heaven and earth came together. The high priest could only enter the Holy of Holies once a year, on the Day of Atonement. During this lone, annual excursion inside the Holy of Holies the high priest would make a blood sacrifice for the sins of all of Israel. The daily, weekly and monthly sacrifices given throughout the year were not sufficient. The final sacrifice was needed.

Jesus Christ replaced this sacrifice and became our perfect gift. Jesus traded places with the high priest, the sacrifice, the blood, the tabernacle and he himself became the Holy of Holies. Jesus became the place where heaven and earth meet and he was the final sacrifice. No further blood need be shed, no mediator need intervene. We placed on Christ our sins past and future and the blood shed by him is sufficient for all.

This perfect gift from God to his chosen people is all man must receive to enter into an eternal relationship with the Lord. No actions or words of man add to or take away from the value of this gift. God gave this gift freely to man and nothing is required of us.

God's eternal love for us is unmatchable. He sent his perfect son to a world saturated with sin to provide us with the gift of eternal life.

☙

"to him who made the great lights, for his steadfast love endures forever;"
- Psalm 136:7

"At Christmas God moved into a very bad neighborhood and began rehabilitating it."
- Tim Keller

PRAY: Holy One of Israel, we thank you for coming to Earth to change our hearts. Your sacrifice was perfect and we can do nothing to add to it. We seek forgiveness for the times where we try to impress others or you by our words, actions or worship. We understand your perfect gift is all we will ever need.

Day #19

Conceived Son

"And Jesus said, 'I am, and you will see the Son of Man seated at the right hand of
Power, and coming with the clouds of heaven.'"
- Mark 14:62

The term "Son of Man" appears 194 in the ESV Bible. It appears over 90 times in
Ezekiel and over 80 times in the Gospels. In the New Testament it is almost always
used when Jesus is talking about himself. He used this term for himself more than any
other. It was a messianic title and clearly pointed to his humanity and the humility of
Christ. It references his everlasting glory, his suffering and his authority during end
times.

In referencing himself as the Son of Man, Jesus is pointing his Jewish listeners to the
prophet Ezekiel's many references to his own humanity. Yet, the term Son of Man
used in Psalms, Daniel, and numerous apocryphal references can be interpreted as
Savior or "made strong." Thus, Christ's use of the term is dualistic in its reference to
his humanity and his salvific nature.

That is what we have in our Son of Man. Jesus was all man and all God at the same
time. His deity was almighty, universal and perfectly good and is humanity got tired,
stubbed his toe, had bad breath and got hungry. Jesus simultaneously possessed the
human experience to relate to our trials and the divine ability to impact our lives.

The judgment and authority of the Son of Man will be as perfect in the end times as
his humanity was 2,000 years ago. The only true perfect man will serve as the only
perfect judge during the end times. The title Son of Man speaks volumes of Jesus.
Only our Messiah could simultaneously and perfectly incorporate all the qualities
encompassed in the unexpectedly complex title of Son of Man.

ଔ

"I saw in the night visions, and behold, with the clouds of heaven there came one
like a son of man, and he came to the Ancient of Days and was presented before
him."
- Daniel 7:13

"Only by his own coming could God's final peace, joy and victory come." - Edmund Clowney

PRAY: Son of Man, your birth and life as a human allows you to have empathy for our sufferings. Your sovereign deity gives you unmatchable wisdom and might to address our needs. We call upon the Son of Man to administer his will, for his glory today, tomorrow and in the end of days.

Earth Dweller

"But will God indeed dwell on the earth? Behold, heaven and the highest heaven
cannot contain you; how much less this house that I have built!"
- 1 Kings 8:27

Solomon finished the construction of the Holy Temple in Jerusalem. The Ark of the
Covenant was moved in and the temple was ready to open. At the dedication
ceremony Solomon stood, with arms raised, before all of Israel and prayed to God. In
the middle of his lengthy prayer over the lavish temple Solomon enquiries to God, if
"heaven cannot contain you; how much less this house that I have built!" It may have
been a little late in the process to inquire about the wisdom of constructing a temple
for God. Nonetheless, 400 years later King Nebuchadnezzar II helped address
questions about God's Temple when he destroyed it during a siege of Jerusalem.
Indeed, God was in the Temple, but he was also simultaneously everywhere else.

God is the Lord of heaven and Earth. He is not shackled to a temple or church.
Temples made by man are wonderful ceremonial dedications to God and can add to
his glory. We must be careful never to envision God is only present in ornate
cathedrals.

God dwells on Earth and his son walked on the same ground we trod today. We must
always remember, God created the Earth for his glory. He populated the Earth with
people he created in his own image. It is not hard to imagine the Lord loves dwelling
among the beauty of his creation.

But, more than for recreational purposes, God dwells on this planet to be close to us
and to commune with his beloved. God also dwells in the perfect and sinless heaven.
Simultaneously, and at all times, he is here, with us. His disciples never need wonder
where their Father is. As you read these words, God is with you.

છ૪

"The God who made the world and everything in it, being Lord of heaven and earth,
does not live in temples made by man,"
- Acts 17:24

"I can't think of anything more pleasing to Christ than the church celebrating his birthday every year." - R.C. Sproul

PRAY: God of heaven and Earth, you love your people and you love the temporary planet you created for us. Help us to see you as simultaneously sitting on your throne in heaven and residing here with us on Earth. You govern from above and are actively involved in our simple daily lives.

Royal Lineage

"The scepter shall not depart from Judah, nor the ruler's staff from between his feet, until tribute comes to him; and to him shall be the obedience of the peoples."
- Genesis 49:10

ꙅ⚬ꙅ

Judah was born 60 years before the words in the passage were spoken, and Christ was born 1,900 years after. Yet the two are connected by lineage and prophecy. At this early point God was already revealing that through Judah's bloodline there would come a royal lineage which would remain unbroken. The line of Judah, the Davidic covenant, the son of David, pointed with historical certainty from where the Messiah would come. From Adam to Noah to Abraham to Judah to David to Rehoboam to Josiah and mercifully to Jesus, God's son.

Jesus was the foretold Lion of the tribe of Judah. When we become disciples of Christ we enter into his family. Through Jesus we are embraced into God's chosen people. As disciples of Christ we become heirs of the covenants and connected back through the history of our fathers, all the way to the Garden of Eden.

In the same way a child who is adopted becomes a legal heir to the estate of his adoptive father, so to do Christians become heirs of the heritage and promises of our fathers before us. The history of Israel becomes our account. The promises of Abraham become our assurances.

As the royal lineage of Jesus is verified in Scripture and he becomes the fulfillment of prophecies our eternal covenant is sealed in his blood. By hitching our eternal wagon to the heir of Judah we watch as his fulfillment of prophecy becomes our undying gain.

Our Savior embodies the keeping of the promises. Jesus descended from Adam, kept the crown in the line of Judah, was born of a virgin, died on a cross and was raised from the grave. Because our Lord ascended and sits at the right hand of God we are heirs to his royal lineage.

ଔ

"And the crowds that went before him and that followed him were shouting, 'Hosanna to the Son of David! Blessed is he who comes in the name of the Lord! Hosanna in the highest!'"
- Matthew 21:9

"Truly, this God is for life, and not just for Christmas!" - Craig Bartholomew

৩৯৫

PRAY: King Forever, your family line is pure and perfect. Your fathers were God's chosen servants and are the fulfillment of countless of God's promises throughout millennia. Help us to value our heredity with you ahead of our own mothers and fathers and sons and daughters. You are our all.

Good Lord

"Like newborn infants, long for the pure spiritual milk, that by it you may grow up into salvation - if indeed you have tasted that the Lord is good."
- 1 Peter 2:2-3

If you have not rested in the goodness and joy of the Lord you must strive for it. To experience God's goodness to its fullest you must put aside pedestrian, lukewarm Christianity and sellout for his glory. You must live all of your life, all for his glory. Don't compartmentalize your faith. The goodness God bestows on you is not the kind of good blessing, promised by bad theology, where God rewards your faith by lavishing you with material wealth. That is man-centered and not Jesus-centered. The goodness of Christ is experienced when you know you are living in his will and you have sacrificed your safety and comfort for his glory. The peace and pure love the Lord gives you when you are completely obedient is more valuable than money and tastes better than fine food.

When disciples of Jesus rest in obedience to the Lord they experience the depth of his grace and goodness. The goodness of Christ, when experienced within a zealous relationship, is like no other sensation. The more you know God's goodness the more you want to live your life enveloped in it.

You who know Christ, once you have tasted his pure spiritual milk, you will long for it even more. Those who are separated from Christ have not had the first taste of his goodness and know not of the void in their hearts. Once you are in Christ and you have experienced the Lord himself, the craving for his goodness is obsessive. You can tell a person who has drawn deeply from the Lord's goodness, they live their days like they never again want to go back a life without it. Don't play at Christianity. Experience his steadfast love like never before and live every part of your life for his glory.

ॐ

"For the LORD is good; his steadfast love endures forever, and his faithfulness to all generations."
- Psalm 100:5

"Man is a sinner who needs an overwhelming love. Jesus has come to save his people from their sins." - Francis Schaeffer

PRAY: Good Shepherd, open our hearts and make us willing to receive your great goodness. It frightens us to relinquish control of our entire life to you, but we want to avail all we have for your will. Help us to step off the ledge and commit to falling deeply in love with your glory.

Eternal Kingdom

"And your house and your kingdom shall be made sure forever before me. Your throne shall be established forever."
- 2 Samuel 7:16

The term "Kingdom of God" appears 67 times in the ESV Bible, all of which occur in the New Testament. While the tem never appears in the Old Testament the concept is present, when God is spoken of as both the King of Israel and of the whole Earth. The Kingdom of God stands as the center of Jesus' message. The Kingdom is both present and future. It is simultaneously the present rule of God and the future realm of Christ.

God's present Kingdom is within us. It requires obedience to God's law and election to his grace. The receiving of the gospel of Christ results in an immediate residency within the Kingdom. The expanding of the bride of Christ grows the Kingdom of God. The present Kingdom rests in the hearts of Christ's disciples and the influence of his blessings.

The coming Kingdom is ushered in by Christ. Jesus instructs us to pray for the coming Kingdom. Both the Gospels and Paul's epistles look forward to a future Kingdom. The eternal Kingdom is still to come and will see Christ at its head.

While we look forward to the joyous coming Kingdom we must not simply view our faith as future promises yet to be fulfilled. In the hearts of men and through his disciples Jesus' Kingdom is an active empire. While our Lord continues to call sinners to himself the Kingdom grows and his glory multiplies.

Jesus was, is and will be the King of the eternal Kingdom. Rejoice in the promises of tomorrow, but live in the magnificence of today. Our Lord and Savior reigns this day and forever more.

☙

"Then the seventh angel blew his trumpet, and there were loud voices in heaven, saying, 'The kingdom of the world has become the kingdom of our Lord and of his Christ, and she shall reign forever and ever.'"
- Revelation 11:15

"God came to earth on Christmas to live, to die, to be raised, to ascend, and to come again. It's all gloriously true." - Kevin DeYoung

PRAY: Author of eternal salvation, you are the Sovereign of our hearts. Your Kingdom is vast and your influence is limitless. The future of your Kingdom does not depend on your subjects, but you command us to play a part in its expansion. Your Kingdom expands, not by force, but by the sharing of your mercies with the lost.

Worshiped King

"Now after Jesus was born in Bethlehem of Judea in the days of Herod the king, behold, wise men from the east came to Jerusalem, saying, 'Where is he who has been born king of the Jews? For we saw his star when it rose and have come to worship him.'"
- Matthew 2:1-2

Theseus was a founding hero of Ancient Greece and King of Athens. He was revered and celebrated. It has been told that Theseus was from a kingly lineage on his mother's side and fathered by the god Poseidon. As a king he helped the poor and ushered in Athenian democracy. He was said to have conquered the Minotaur and completed many adventures depicted in books, plays and film. The escapades of Theseus are legendary. Mythology, history and art knit together an amazing man. In the end, the much adored Theseus, was exiled from his beloved Athens, and died alone. In both fact and fiction, Theseus was a great king. In the end, he perished as all men do.

Our King entered the world surrounded by farm animals and began his death march by being brought into town on the back of a lowly donkey. While on Earth he did not wear a crown of gold, nor did he dine with powerful men. Jesus did not sit on a throne ordained in jewels and did not wear fine clothes. Our Lord was the most significant king in history and today wields power surpassing the combined force of all leaders, past and present.

Our humble King of the Universe is the most significant of all. Our King is worshiped not because of his physical force or fear. Our King is worshiped because he is the ultimate servant. Christ does not conquer with force; he transforms with love.

We are called to respect and honor the human leaders of the world, yet, never forget our ultimate governing authority rests is Jesus. Our King is worshiped because he is the originator of grace, mercy and justice. Our King is eternal.

◈

"Rejoice greatly, O daughter of Zion! Shout aloud, O daughter of Jerusalem! Behold, your king is coming to you; righteous and having salvation is he, humble and mounted on a donkey"
- Zechariah 9:9

"The name Emmanuel takes in the whole mystery. Jesus is 'God with us.' He had a nature like our own in all things, sin only excepted. But though Jesus was 'with us' in human flesh and blood, He was at the same time very God." - J.C. Ryle

PRAY: King of Israel, you are humble and all-powerful. You are an unachievable standard by which all leaders are compared. Your disciples follow you not in fear, but in love. We worship our King who is worthy. Give us hearts which burn to share your majesty with the world.

Excellent Mediator

"But as it is, Christ has obtained a ministry that is as much more excellent than the old as the covenant he mediates is better, since it is enacted on better promises."
- Hebrews 8:6

ço∞

In God's predestination of man, all of creation benefits from the Lord's glorious blessings and provision while on Earth. In God's great mercy he allows all of mankind to benefit from his blessings whether they acknowledge his majesty or not. Upon death, God's elect receive mercy and commune with their Savior while the reprobate are served justice and are separated from God's love. No man who ever desired a relationship with the Father has ever been denied salvation by the Lord. All of us are sinners and deserve the justice of eternal punishment, yet some receive unearned mercy and are elect for salvation. God's predestination of man is like a summer thunderstorm during a drought. Everyone enjoys the fruit produced by the merciful rain which falls on the dry soil, yet during the storm, some are coaxed out to dance in the rain while others are left to embrace their true nature and hide from the thunder.

As our sovereign Lord choose to love Jacob and hate Esau, in his infinite wisdom he deems it appropriate to choose some sinners for an eternity in heaven and others for eternity in hell. Our astonishment should not rest in the reality that some are sent to hell, but that any are sent to heaven. We all deserve hell. In his great knowledge and by his great mercy he allows some of the unworthy to be pardoned of their sins.

The wonders of God were not all meant for us to comprehend in this life. Our purpose, as his creation, is to embrace his clear teachings in Scripture and give him constant glory. Our perfect and sovereign Mediator performs many mercies which are beyond our capacity. Praise be to the Lord, his perfect will is done.

ଔ

"There is no arbiter between us, who might lay his hand on us both."
- Job 9:33

"Who can add to Christmas? The perfect motive is that God so loved the world. The perfect gift is that He gave His only Son. The only requirement is to believe in Him. The reward of faith is that you shall have everlasting life." - Corrie Ten Boom

PRAY: Jesus, Mediator of the new covenant, we would rather have no other be the ultimate judge of man. We rejoice at knowing you intercede for man so your chosen can commune with the Father. Thank you for intervening in our eternity where we possess neither the foreknowledge nor the will to choose on our own.

Virgin Born

"Therefore the Lord himself will give you a sign. Behold, the virgin shall conceive and
bear a son, and shall call his name Immanuel."
- Isaiah 7:14

The doctrine of the virgin birth claims Jesus was conceived in Mary without the involvement of a human father. Muslims believe this to be true. According to Newsweek, 79% of all Americans believe Christ was born of a virgin, without a human father. John Calvin declared Jesus, "was pleased to be conceived miraculously in the Virgin's womb." Billy Graham stated Christ was "born of a virgin." But, is it really that important?

Some people believe in Christ but not the virgin birth. Somehow turning water to wine or raising the dead is an easy enough miracle, but, being born of a virgin is too farfetched. If Jesus' grand exit, rising from the dead and ascending to heaven, is miraculous, why would his entrance into the world be any less astonishing?

Nearly 800 years before Jesus was born, Isaiah wrote, "Therefore the Lord himself will give you a sign. Behold, the virgin shall conceive and bear a son, and shall call his name Immanuel." In order to fulfill prophecy, Christ had to be born of a virgin. If Jesus was not born of a virgin, he was not the Savior of man.

The Old Testament foretold the Messiah would be born to a virgin and in Matthew and Luke the Bible confirms that indeed Jesus was born of a virgin. The Bible is the literal, infallible Word of God. To deny the virgin birth is to deny the perfection of God and his perfect Scriptures. If the Creator of the Universe desired to be born to a virgin, and says that he was, it is then imperative we, as his loving disciples, embrace the historical fact of the virgin birth.

ℭℜ

"And Mary said to the angel, 'How will this be, since I am a virgin?'"
- Luke 1:34

"And it was our Lord and Savior Jesus Christ, the true and only eternal Son of God, who had to be sent and given to mankind by the Father, to restore a world otherwise wasted, destroyed, and desolate." - John Calvin

PRAY: Firstborn of all creation, you always have been and always will be. Your miraculous birth, life, death and resurrection declare you the fulfiller of prophecy and worthy of our dying adoration. We are pleased to worship you as you are, not as we desire you to be.

Joyful Reconciler

"And when the LORD smelled the pleasing aroma, the LORD said in his heart, 'I will never again curse the ground because of man, for the intention of man's heart is evil from his youth. Neither will I ever again strike down every living creature as I have done.'"
- Genesis 8:21

⤜⤛

Domesticated parrots are highly intelligent animals. Some have been known to have vocabularies exceeding several hundred words. But, even though these birds are intelligent, they are prone to self-mutilation. Parrots are so fixated on cleaning themselves, that if a parrot is not distracted it can harm or even kill itself. Parrots preen, pluck feathers, pick at their skin and attempt to remove their imperfections. Though a parrot is highly intelligent they have been known to clean themselves to death. Even with the best of intentions some parrots simply can't refrain from doing what they know is wrong.

The heart of man is so completely and utterly permeated with sin, that left to his own devices man would never choose goodness. Because of his natural and complete commitment to sin, man would never select to honor God on his own. Our mutiny against God is complete. On his own, man can only sin. Even when his actions are good, his intent is sinful.

Human sin and the complete corruption of our hearts absolutely warrants our eternal damnation. The only naturally occurring good in the world is God. The depraved heart of man cannot choose God, because God is good. Without God opening our hearts and giving us our faith we would be eternally separated from him.

Man's heart is evil, but Christ chooses to soften the heart of some and gives them a new heart inclined toward him. The perfect child, born without sin came to a sinful world to save a bankrupt people. The birth of Christ, for the first time, ushered in the ability for man's heart to experience goodness.

ଔ

"One who heard us was a woman named Lydia, from the city of Thyatira, a seller of purple goods, who was a worshiper of God. The Lord opened her heart to pay attention to what was said by Paul."
- Acts 16:14

"A prison cell, in which one waits, hopes…and is completely dependent on the fact that the door of freedom has to be opened from the outside, is not a bad picture of Advent." - Dietrich Bonhoeffer

PRAY: Shaddai, you are good and sinless and perfect. We are not. You have cleansed us of the eternal effects of sin like a vaccination. The sinful heart of man loves to covet his own safety and comfort. Thank you Lord for giving us the ability to be aware of our sin and to long for you.

Personal Savior

"For unto you is born this day in the city of David a Savior, who is Christ the Lord."
- Luke 2:11

A man was walking along a seashore at low tide. The sand was littered with thousands of beached and dying starfish. As he kept walking the man came across a small boy throwing one starfish at a time into the ocean. The man said, "Son, this is a waste of time. There are so many starfish on the beach. You can never make a difference." Without looking up from his task the boy picked up another starfish and threw it into the ocean. Still looking out at the water, the boy said, "I made a difference for that one."

The all-powerful God of all is a Creator who is beyond measure. Yet, this infinite, all-knowing being recognizes you by name and cares deeply about that which troubles you. It is hard to grasp, but this God of everything wants to have an individual relationship with you and be your personal Savior.

When Jesus was born, he did not come for a people group or a nation. He came for you. Jesus became a man to pay for your sins and to reconcile you to God. He is a personal Savior and desires to spend an eternity with you. Jesus came to Earth and suffered under humiliation to bring you into his covenant family.

Embrace your personal Savior with the intimate and loving relationship he desires. God is too big for us to comprehend, but he is not too big to love you personally and have your name on his lips. God is worthy of reverence and respect, but he is not swayed with ceremony and flowery speech. Cherish your relationship with God and show him the warm affection worthy of the closest relationship you'll ever know.

ᘓ

"For to us a child is born, to us a son is given; wand the government shall be upon his shoulder, and his name shall be called Wonderful Counselor, Mighty God, Everlasting Father, Prince of Peace."
- Isaiah 9:6

"All those who find salvation will be saved by the atoning work of Jesus the Christ, the virgin-born Savior." - Albert Mohler

PRAY: our just God and Savior, we seek to know you more. It is our desire to honor and respect you, but not to put you so far out of reach that we will never comprehend you. Teach us to not be afraid to imagine you could diminish yourself so much that you could desire a personal relationship with us.

Nation Gatherer

"And to him was given dominion and glory and a kingdom, that all peoples, nations, and languages should serve him; his dominion is an everlasting dominion, which shall not pass away, and his kingdom one that shall not be destroyed."
- Daniel 7:14

The groundbreaking nineteenth century missionary to inland China, Hudson Taylor, was a great servant of God. Taylor was not great because of anything good in him, but because he knew that, "Christ is either Lord of all, or He is not Lord at all." Yet, Taylor struggled like other missionaries. While on the mission field he lost six children and two wives. Through his suffering he held fast to the fact that knowledge of our Savior necessitated Christians reaching out to the lost. Taylor said, "The Great Commission is not an option to be considered; it is a command to be obeyed." The only response to our knowledge of grace and mercy of Christ is to share his gospel with the lost.

Our God is a missionary God and desires the lost throughout the world to be reconciled with him. He commands his disciples to reach out to those who do not know him. Each of us is to participate in the sharing of the gospel with the lost across the street and around the world. We participate in missions and evangelism not because we are super Christians, because we are obedient Christians.

We brag of our love for our favorite politician, sports team or musical artist. We should spread the joy of Christ even more fervently. Sharing the gospel is not another church ministry to choose from, it is the heart of the church. Our love for our Savior and his desire for the lost compels obedient Christians to share the gospel.

The mercy and grace God has bestowed upon you is best savored when it is shared with the lost Christ has placed in your path. Tell the world of God's great love by starting with the next person you meet.

ℭℜ

"And Jesus came and said to them, 'All authority in heaven and on earth has been given to me. Go therefore and make disciples of all nations, baptizing them in the name of the Father and of the Son and of the Holy Spirit, teaching them to observe all that I have commanded you. And behold, I am with you always, to the end of the age.'"
- Matthew 28:18-20

"This baby in a manger is worthy. He is worthy of adoration as the sinless Savior, born on Christmas to die for sinners." - David Platt

PRAY: Light of the Nations, the historical fact of your birth, death and resurrection is simply too miraculous to keep to ourselves. Help us to reach out to the lost, not because we love them, but because we love you. You have not asked your disciples, but commanded us, to share your gospel. Use us to bring yourself glory.

Index of passages by Bible book, chapter and verse:

Printed in Great Britain
by Amazon

50831905R00043